All The Things I Never Said

Written by Jennie Louise

Illustrated by Gina Stavrou

All rights reserved. This book (or any portion thereof) may not be reproduced or used in any manner without the written permission of the author, except for brief quotations in critical articles or reviews.

ISBN: 9798693912274

Copyright © 2020 by Jennie Louise

Illustrations copyright © 2020 by Gina Stavrou

Contents

To Family

Tiny Dancer	8
I Hold the Sky in My Hands	9
Forget-Me-Not	10
Soft Touches Burn Too	12
Emotionally Unavailable	13
I Shouldn't, But I Do	14
Somewhere	15
The Smell of Nostalgia	16
In Search of the World	18
Sunshine Lullabies	19

To Lovers

When We Were Young	22
Colours	23
Coffee Doesn't Burn Like You Do	24
The Difference Between Sex and Making Love	26
Coping Mechanisms	27
You Aren't the Same You I See in my Dreams	28
A Letter to my Last Lover	30
Nothing is Okay	32
Body Language	34
One More Day	35

To Strangers

Dawn	38
Message in a Bottle	39
Cherry Blossom	40
The House in Your Head	41
Dried-Out Pens	42
Amidst Silence	43
Red	44
The Melancholy Nature of Winter	45
Blue Glow	46
Wanderer	48

To Myself

Tough to Be A Bug	52
Mosaic of Memories	53
Lotus	54
People Like Me	55
The Pessimist's Eyes	56
One, Two, Ten	57
Behind Closed Doors	58
Grieving Myself	60
Simplicity	61
Eternity	62

To Family

Tiny Dancer

Do you remember the time
we were driving back from the airport at 5am?
The sun was rising, sky of pinky blue
cotton ball clouds; the roads empty,
our skin like toffee, sun-kissed;
morning coffee on our lips.
Tiny dancer was playing on the radio.
Windows down, volume up;
Cool air keeping my eyes awake,
Running through my hair;
Singing lyrics at the top of our voices,
Foot on the pedal driving the straight roads
towards home. When you hear that song,
do you remember how the morning felt,
who was by your side? Or
have you forgotten me already?

I Hold the Sky in My Hands

I have been angry since I was 12.
Clenched fists so tight,
my nails left half-moons in my palms.
I wasn't allowed to be angry,
but held the sky in my hands
as stars exploded across the skin.
Oh, how it burned, but it was better
than letting you know I had suffered.
It has been years and my palms still sting.
I ache with anger.

Forget-Me-Not

I was drawing gravestones
when I should have been drawing flowers,
Crafting nooses from
daisy chains rather than crowns,
Pulling petals (he loves me,
he loves me not)
off roses stolen from neighbours' gardens
because no one bought them
for each other in our house.
I learned to press flowers in books,
desperate to preserve
a beauty that didn't exist
until I left home (you).
My father was the first man
to break my heart, leaving me
to wonder why they were called forget-me-nots
when I was so often forgotten.
I didn't understand why people bought flowers
if they were only going to die;
Nothing stays beautiful forever
but maybe a bouquet can
brighten a broken family
more than a child can.

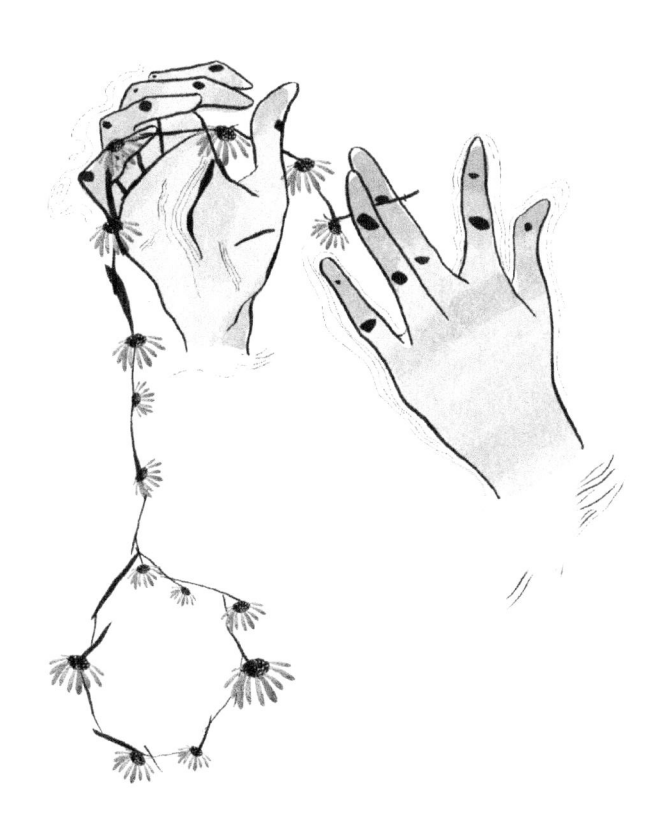

Soft Touches Burn Too

Your touch is soft but it burns,
Leaving red handprints upon the skin
that fade as if they were never there.
But they *were* there.
Every time you gripped my body, your hand
wrapped around my skinny wrist
as the other came down against my thigh
where lava flooded and cooled,
a mould of your palm left on the surface.
Skin so hot I couldn't feel the cold
tears running down my face, hitting
the burn and bringing me more comfort
than you ever did.
You don't slap me anymore but
I still hear skin hitting skin
like a cracker bursting over Christmas dinner,
A balloon popping on my birthday.
None of it compares to the heat in your eyes,
your face as red as the mark on my body.
I still flinch at sudden movements.
Burns fade but they don't disappear;
They leave scars in the shape of handprints.

Emotionally Unavailable

You're ignoring me again.
I split myself down the middle to
share my deepest emotions:
Rub my eyes until they're red raw,
Wet eyelashes glued to my cheeks,
Spiders legs, my insides crawl from me.
Keep pretending I'm not there,
Because if I acknowledge your silence
I might just explode
in an eruption of tears and guts;
a stain on the carpet for you
to walk through when you leave.

I Shouldn't, But I Do

I shouldn't have to force myself
to cry for you to know that I'm suffering,
that it's real and it hurts.
I'm not much of a crier;
Raised by a mother that forbid it
like she was in turn, we learned
to bury the tears in a locked box
labelled weak, childish, unladylike.
I have more tears in that box
than times I have felt sad
because tears aren't just for the melancholy.
They're for the angry, the lonely,
the resentful and the happy (sometimes).
I shouldn't have to hurt myself
to prove that I'm in pain but
I do, I do, I do.

Somewhere

Six years ago, we rented a cottage
in the middle of nowhere,
Just us, living life in the wilderness.
The first evening we lay on our backs
in the long grass, staring at the sky.
It took a while for our eyes to adjust,
But when they did, stars appeared
with each new blink, scattering
the black like paint splashes.
Blades of grass swayed in the silent
breeze beneath my fingertips,
Your hand rested in mine,
Squeezing each time a star shot
across the blackness.
Now when I feel alone, I lie in bed
swearing I can still feel
the gentle touch of your hand.
But it is only when I open my eyes,
that I am faced with the ceiling
and an empty space beside me.

The Smell of Nostalgia

If I had a candle for every smell
that ignited my mind with forgotten memories,
They would sit in a shop, row by row,
Waiting for someone to reminisce
in their nostalgia.
The smell of my mother's washing powder
as I sat amongst her clothes
in the bottom of the wardrobe, silent
and waiting to be found.
The brand of hairspray that fogged the room
as I backcombed my hair for a night out.
The aftershave my first boyfriend
wore to every date or special occasion.
That new car smell and the smell of an empty
house, ready to become a home.
A freshly mown lawn on a spring Sunday
with the roast dinner wafting.
The first perfume I bought myself after my heart
was broken, lasting long enough for me
to learn to love myself again.
The candles don't get much business;
Nobody seems to understand the smells like I do.
But that's okay, it isn't for them anyway.

In Search of the World

I left home in search of the world,
Only to realise that it was in my mother's lap
with her fingers running through my hair.

Sunshine Lullabies

Leaves whisper around my feet
as they rustle and blow in circles, humming
in tune to your voice as you sing
lullabies about the sunshine.
The smallness of my hand in yours, gripping,
Hurrying to keep up:
Tiny legs in tiny boots,
Pops of pink in the grass like candy buttons
on my coat, done up to the chin.
Before I know it, you are gone
and there's a new little girl whose hand
is soft like petals in mine.
I dare to feel young again, rosy
cheeks blurred as my own child
cartwheels in the grass.
The leaves still whisper around my feet,
the sound of sunshine
on my lips.

To Lovers

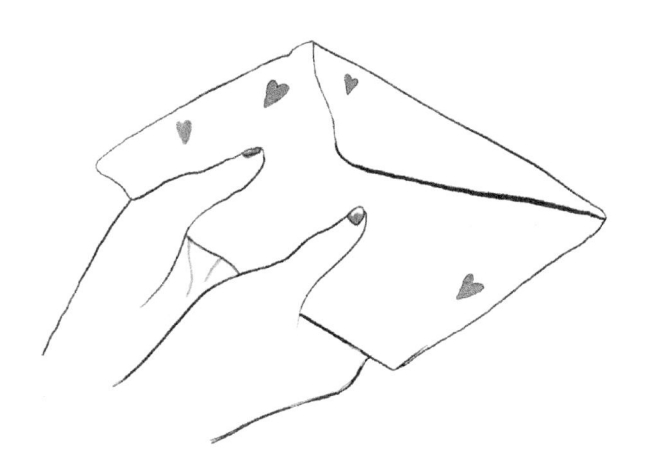

When We Were Young

When we were young
you begged me to write about you:
a poem dedicated to our romance
that you saw through rose-tinted glasses.
I couldn't do it, not then.
Now it's been years and I'm back
in that place where we began;
Walking the same streets and sitting
in the same park, the one with our names
scratched into the bench.
You wanted a love like those in movies.
I hope you've found it now.
But if you haven't,
here's the poem you wanted
back when we were young.

Colours

It was red:
sloppy kisses, hands on my thighs,
lips tasting of cinnamon.

It was orange:
eyes after smoking a pack of cigarettes
in an empty car park.

It was yellow:
sour sweets and home-made lemonade,
sugar fizzing on our tongues.

It was green:
plants we forgot to water,
too busy pouring ourselves into each other.

It was blue:
overflowing streets during a storm,
dirty paint water ready to be thrown out.

It was indigo:
bruises like a map on my neck
from someone that wasn't you.

It was violet:
all neon lights, sitting in late night cafés
writing poetry until my fingers went numb.

Coffee Doesn't Burn Like You Do

I wasn't good at love.
And you weren't good at sticking around.
There was nothing beautiful about it;
I fell into you like rain hits the ground,
Non-stop, hard and fast, all at once.
Your lips were like hot coffee,
Burning my tongue because I loved you
too much to be patient.
My lips still tingle when I think about your taste.
I tried to stop myself
from dripping into your coffee,
but you stubbed me out like your last cigarette.
I never claimed to be good at any of this.
You never said you'd stay.

The Difference Between Sex and Making Love

I'm lonely for love and sick of sex.
Wasting time on meaningless encounters
spent giving myself to strangers
who only want my body.
I want to have sex with someone
I love; where it's more
than skin to skin
but mind to mind.
I'm fed up of finishing
when they are done and I'm not,
Having to get dressed in silence
and sneak out before the shame sinks in.
I want to fall asleep naked and warm,
where the feeling of being held
brings safety, not constraint.

Coping Mechanisms

I remember how the moon looked
on the day we met.
Sat on my window ledge
listening to leaves curl and crunch
in a rusted dance, hidden by darkness
as clouds passed overhead.
I couldn't escape the thought of you,
Writing lame poems and hoping
that you were thinking of me too.
The moon looks the same tonight
as it did on that day.
I'm still listening to the leaves
and watching the clouds
but I burned all the poetry I wrote
about you. Except this one.

You Aren't the Same You I See in my Dreams

You came to my dreams again last night.
Although it looked like you,
It wasn't the you I knew.
This 'you' was soft to touch,
with lips that roamed my body
like the silk bedsheets wrapped around me.
This 'you' was forgiving,
With your cheek against the pillow
you listened to my words as if they
were made of gold.
This 'you' fell asleep with your limbs
intertwined with mine,
Feeding off my warmth as our lids
became heavy, breath became steady.
I was scared to open my eyes this morning:
I knew yours wouldn't be looking back at me.
Yet I was certain I could smell you
on my pillow, my clothes, my skin,
as if you had been there
the night before.

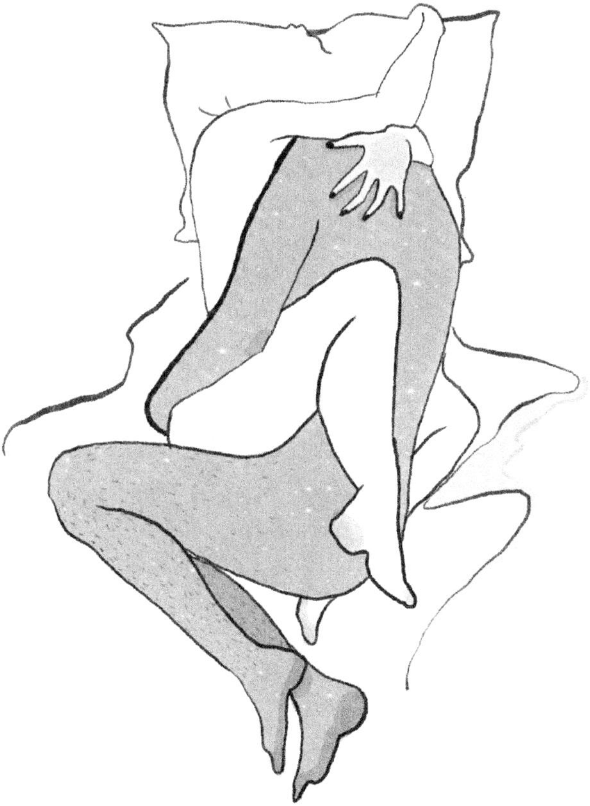

A Letter to my Last Lover

This is not a love letter.
Only words on paper
that say everything I never could.
I don't love you anymore
but being alone is hard
and it's even harder watching you
move on with someone new.
How could you forget me
when your side of the bed is still warm?
The feelings are gone but I remember
the way my stomach churned
like bubbles dance in champagne:
Rising, floating, settling.
Only the ache remains
(not the ache of wanting you,
I have moved past that) but
the ache of love.
Loving someone and being loved in return.
I wonder, do you think about me?
Are there times when you miss me too?
How about my body in bed?

Probably best if you don't answer those.
I know someone else shares your bed
but does she kiss your neck like I did?
Don't answer that either.
I keep saying I'm over you
(and I am) but I'm not over
the idea of you.
Does it even matter? Did I ever?
This is not a love letter; I don't love you
anymore but I wish I did.

Nothing is Okay

It's not okay that we don't talk anymore.
That we shared so much in the time we had
and still returned to strangers
despite promising that we wouldn't.
It's not okay that I'm still friends
with your mum and your sister,
That I think of them as the family I never had.
It's not okay that I remember your birthday
with each passing year, desperate
to send you my best wishes.
It's not okay that I look at your horoscope
before I read my own,
knowing that this month will bring you
stability and me nostalgia.
It's not okay that I remember our anniversary;
The way the trees talked
when we laid our heads in the grass
and it's not okay that sometimes,
when I'm really longing,
I go back to that place to find the grass
is dried up and the trees don't talk anymore.
It's not okay.

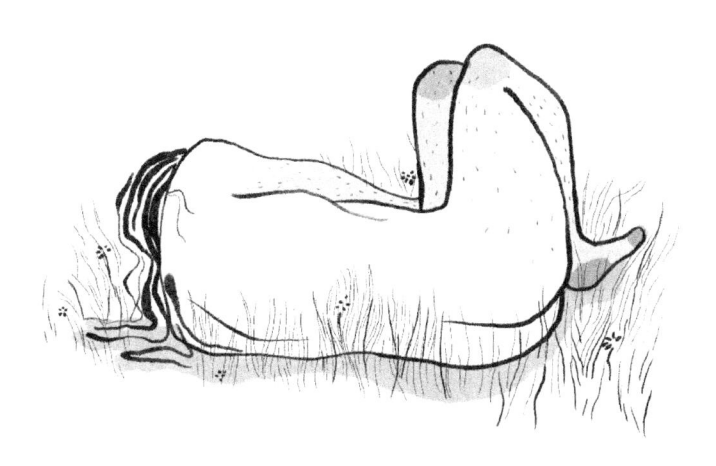

Body Language

If we were to meet again,
what would we say to one another?
Would our bodies do the talking
like they used to:
the brush of fingertips as we walked
close enough to grasp but never reaching out.
Or would we force our mouths to talk
polite nothings while we
buried the words we were always
too scared to say, not realising
that they escaped in other ways;
your eyes were always easier
to read than your lips.

One More Day

Could you have loved me one more day?
I know I could have loved you
for as many days as you wanted me.
Things ended too fast. I tried
to keep you but you were already gone:
Asleep with your eyes open,
Distant as you gazed beyond
the figure standing before you.
I wish we'd had more time
so I could have proved
that I was worth keeping,
Even if it was just for one more day.

To Strangers

Dawn

Light streams through open windows
casting yellow pools on white bedsheets.
The sky is orange with a new dawn
like fresh apricots and you lay beside me,
breathing softly with sleep.
I pray that all mornings are like this;
where the sun is as thick as honey
and dreams are as light as clouds.

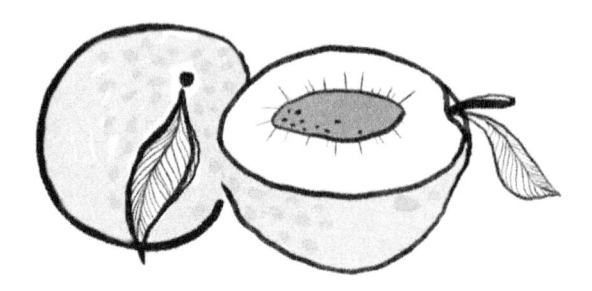

Message in a Bottle

A dreamer of lands beyond the Bermuda Triangle
writes words of silk from pale fingertips,
a twisted tornado filled with messages
from the mind. Released,
bobbing with the current
that carries it weightlessly.

The further it goes to sea,
the heavier the words become, disintegrating
into stones of burden.
The bottle cannot withstand the density
of the message it carries
It fades and falters among the waves until

saltwater seeps into glass, crinkling
the paper and blurring the lines.
Only the dreamer knows the truth.
Gurgles ripple as the message is consumed;
Another empty bottle embedded in the sand,
carrying words too heavy to float.

Cherry Blossom

A bud, pink like flushed cheeks
from winter air, soft flesh,
each petal growing in its own way
with creases that fold and overlap, wet
from morning dew that leaves its stain
as lightly as the touch leaves
goose bumps on the skin.
Moisture seeps from its edges
like the juice from the first bite
of a fruit; peach, papaya:
it does not matter which,
only that with each unfolding petal
and each ripple that cascades down its stem,
does it finally blossom.

The House in Your Head

I want to live in the house inside your head.
I'll paint the walls blue;
Not like the sky but periwinkle, soft
and breezy like thoughts drifting in and out
of open windows.
I'll pick fresh flowers from the garden
and pot them in the vase on the dinner table,
the one beneath the pink and white check
tablecloth your Mum gave you.
When it gets dark, I'll light the fire,
lie on the grass and watch shooting stars.
I'll fall asleep in your bed
with a hundred pillows because I know
you like to feel like you're floating.
I'll always wait for you
to return and while I do, I'll tend
to that house inside your mind.

Dried-Out Pens

I've sat at a desk countless times
and stared at a blank computer screen,
held a pen in my hand that left the paper
as empty as my head.
It would bend and flow like wet paintbrushes
but my brain's regressed back to childhood:
Dried out like pen tips that
lost their lids,
Words escaping in gibberish.
Some days I burst with inspiration
but when I pick up the pencil it snaps
and when I pick up a crayon it cracks.
I'm holding too tight, pressing too hard,
I'm squeezed dry like a sponge without water,
Hardened like paint at the bottom of the tube;
Oh, where can my creativity be?

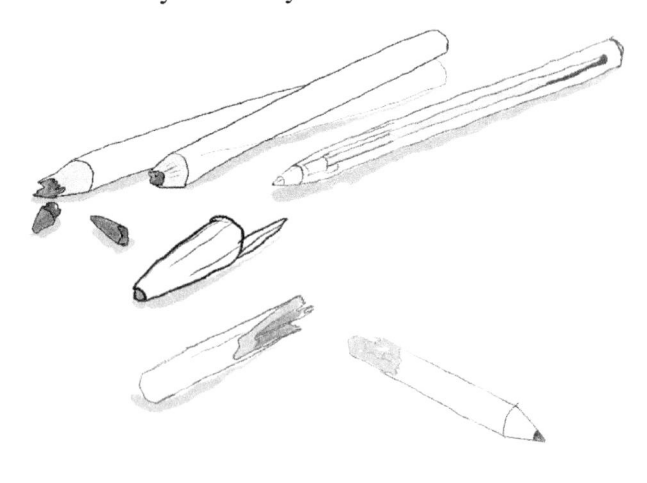

Amidst Silence

You said you wanted to hear
my thoughts. I'm sorry
that I'm empty, alone
in the void inside my head
Floating in nowhere, somewhere,
a place unknown even to me.
I live entirely in my imagination;
Gone but not forgotten,
I keep myself company.
The world is so loud
but amidst the silence
there is nothing and everything
all at once;
A stillness that creates the comfort
I need to save myself.
You wouldn't understand that.

Red

She was red like lipstick stains on pints of beer.
He was red too, but not the romantic kind;
The popping red pills kind, dropping them
when she turns away kind.
She was red like bruised knees against tiles
in a public bathroom where he tilted her head
to meet more red.
He was like headlights, blinding red
as she stumbled home, bare foot and alone,
heels in hand.
She was red smeared from cuts on her soles
as she climbed into an empty bathtub,
Red like her skin once she'd scrubbed his lasting
scent from every inch of her.

The Melancholy Nature of Winter

As I walk down the archway, branches seem to move,
Twisting and curling, blocking out the
misted sky. The world is monochrome;
The arms of the trees like bone.
Cracked bark and wasted moss join
like an antique owner mending a broken doll;
A hole of darkness in her face of glass.
There isn't just one hand, but dozens,
Adjusting themselves in the sky as they bend closer,
Crooked and stiff, intertwining
with wisps of hair, stroking my arms.
They do not welcome me.
Pulling my hair and pushing me forward,
My footsteps turn into a run. I don't look back
until the archway opens, where darkness separates.
I can see the sky once more.
When I turn, there are no hands beckoning me:
The bones against my skin were only the
branches of trees after winter.

Blue Glow

We meet at the same time each week;
Two strangers whose paths cross
in a space where time does not exist.
Each Wednesday, I arrive first.
Streetlights illuminate like eyes
in the shadows as I sit in the fluorescent
blue glow of the laundromat
waiting, waiting for you.
When you arrive, I watch you
load the same machine as always,
The rhythmic humming soothing the silence
as we sit in opposite corners.
You pull out a different book from last week
(Moby Dick) and I watch you
turn the pages, blissfully unaware of my stare.
Clothes spin like rag dolls, I swear
there are bubbles in my ears crackling
like tissue paper. I'm desperate
to speak to you, anything,
(nice weather, isn't it?)
but I can't find the courage. Maybe
I left it in the pocket of my jeans,
The pair with the hole in the knee,
The pair inside the machine
which has now stopped.

The humming is heavier as I take
my clothes with one last look
(your eyes don't lift from the pages).
I leave the blue gloom for the night air,
Anticipating the next Wednesday
I see you, wondering which book you'll have then.

Wanderer

The sky is black
and it's raining flowers.
I wander an endless city
where the only light is the glow
of streetlamps and far away windows;
Like fireflies, they lead me to nowhere.
My feet follow the dusting
of petals that litter the ground
like shards of glass from a broken teacup.
I am okay with having no destination.

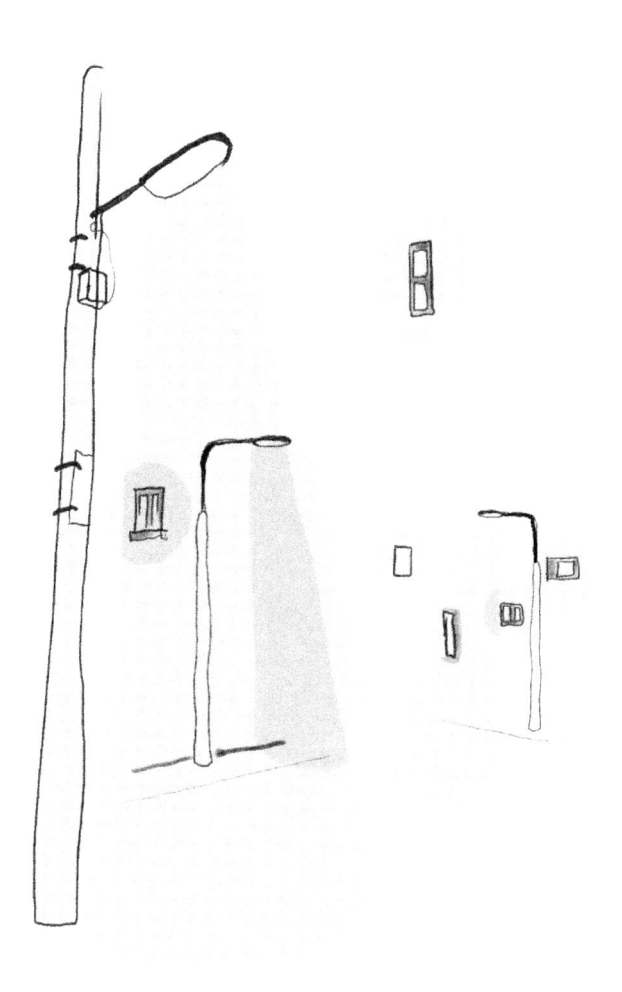

To Myself

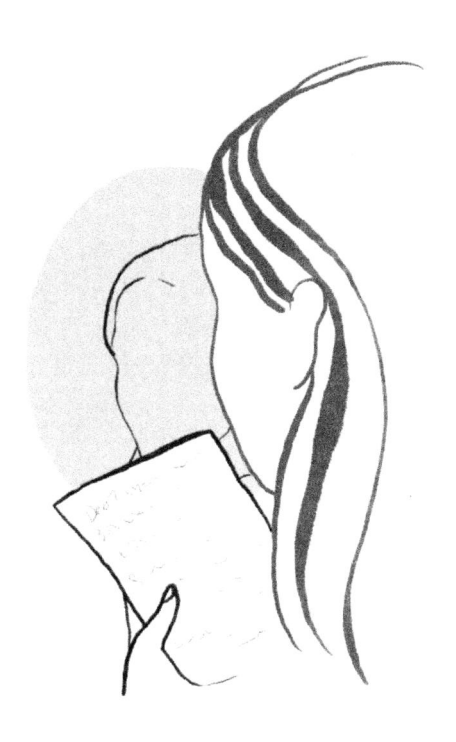

Tough to Be A Bug

As a child, I wondered how ants survived
when they were so small
and my feet were so big.
I spent years looking down,
Desperately trying not to step
on the creatures that fascinated me so.
One day, I saw children in the street
pour boiling water down cracks in the pavement,
into an ant's nest where the dust crumbled
as millions of black dots scattered.
I had never seen so many ants in one place,
so many without a home.
I cried all afternoon, wondering
how tough it must be to be a bug.

Mosaic of Memories

Our lives are made up of people
like glass shards in a mosaic;
Some parts remain long after the person leaves.
My PIN number is still my primary school
best friend's birthday.
There are people I don't talk to anymore
whose families are still in my prayers.
I know all the lyrics to a song me
and the girls from my street
made a dance routine to when we were twelve.
There's a collection of oversized T-shirts
from ex-lovers that I still wear to bed.
(some are married now, some have kids.)
I remember the way my friend's brother
takes his tea (milk, no sugar)
and that his favourite colour is green.
I still haven't found a macaroni cheese
recipe that is better than my
university flatmates'.
Just as these things make up the mosaic
of my life, it's comforting to think
that there are so many lives I have become
a part of, that I have no idea about.

Lotus

It's dark where I am.
Nothing surrounds me but muddy water
pushing; I sway with my roots in the ground.
It's a burden on my shoulders,
Dragging me down into the depths of darkness.
There's a light in the distance,
A passage taking me to a new world
that is full of colour and beauty.
I use all my strength to rise,
feeling lighter until

I erupt from the water like an opening palm.
I am the colour of pink bloom, delicate
and fragile on the outside but inside
I grew from the bottom of the earth,
smothered by dirt; no longer
will I be kept hidden.
Bright like morning,
The air is as clean as crystals
and I know that here
is where I'm meant to be.

People Like Me

I don't think I was made for love;
For the joy or the corniness
or the heartbreak when it ends,
Because it is always bound to end
for someone like me.
I obsess over love, dreaming of
versions of people that don't exist anymore,
The layer of skin they shed kept inside
a heart shaped locket by my bedside.
I'm trapped in the memories,
Replaying them like a stuck record
until the pictures don't look like pictures
and the voices don't sound like us anymore.
People like me weren't made for
the kind of love that lasts a lifetime;
We're too busy loving the ghosts of people
that wander in and out of our minds
just as they did our lives.

The Pessimist's Eyes

People tell me I'm too negative.
I need to cheer up and smile more
but I know better.
Expecting the worst is my speciality
when people are prone to morphing
into the person they promised to protect
you from.
I'll never be disappointed again.
Too many times have I been the cause
of my own pain, raising my hopes
only for them to be crushed
under the weight of my ability to trust.
Vulnerability is a fool's game
where the weapon is used against
you because you gave it to them.
Just once it would be nice to be
the optimistic one,
But being negative comes easier to me
than happiness does;
and that's the saddest part of all.

One, Two, Ten

One, two, ten.
Hourglasses of fate that prove
it can only be a matter of time before I shatter.
Sharp and transparent, I cut myself
with a razor-sharp piece of my own
broken heart, the blade
as poignant as the smashed fragments
across the floor.
Spectrum of colours I hold in my palm,
They strangle me until I am powerless,
grasping and clutching at nothing.
On my tongue they fizz and crackle,
Burning my throat like vodka. They fall into
the bottomless pit, rotting
in my stomach with the other anomalies
from before and before.
I'm suffocating on pendulums, a time-bomb
ticking. I know these will not be the last.
I take again
one, two, ten.

Behind Closed Doors

After I killed myself
my bedroom became a time capsule.
An unmade bed, pyjamas on the floor,
Shelves full of books I was going to read
someday but never will.
Dried wax pooled around half-burnt
candles that lost their smell,
beside empty photo frames waiting
to be filled.
Plants I had spent so long trying
to keep alive, wilted
as dust settled on their leaves.
Old cards from years past
sat on the window, edges curled.
A desk as messy as my mind
holds snippets from magazines
that I planned to make into art,
to-do lists and shopping lists,
empty notebooks and letters
stained by my handwriting.
Everything I left stayed behind,
Except me.

Grieving Myself

I've been grieving the old me.
The little girl with a lion's mane
of flyaway hairs, running
so fast her heels never touched the floor,
always lost in her own world of stories.
She was stabbed in the back,
Losing years of imagination
that would have kept her sane.
To this day, the knife is still in my back,
Ready for the malicious hand that
twists it, reminding me that I'm beyond
repair and the old me is never coming back.

Simplicity

I am a multitude of simplicities:
I am the skies I have admired,
the early morning sunrises and star-stricken nights;
The flowers I've picked and those received;
I am the books I've read, the words
that seeped through my fingertips;
The tears I've cried, left stained on my pillow
and the laughter that echoed like music.
I am moulded by cosmic stardust,
the descendent of my ancestors.
There is nothing simple about me,
for I am a concoction of all I have lived
and all I have learned.

Eternity

Bury me among the flower beds
where the earth is soft like bedsheets.
I do not wish for a grave, only for my pale skin to
blend with the blackness of the soil as I rot.
Flowers will welcome me with open arms,
Their leaves growing over my body, adding colour
to my monochrome soul. They will stroke
the layers from my skin, dropping them
with their own petals so
I can be free like wind-blown dandelions puffs.

Bury me with the insects that are friendlier
than humanity, who will accept me for who I am,
not what I pretend to be.
They will creep across my chilled organs
and decompose my insides.
Maggots will roam freely while worms in my brain
remove all knowledge with their poison;
It will flood from my empty eyes,
Until everything in my body is as hollow
as it was before I was born.

Bury me so I can disintegrate into the earth
with nothing left of my existence but my bones,
ghostly between the blooming flowers and grass
which will become my home beneath the soil.
My body will feed the dirt with its nutrients
as roots and shoots grow once more.
I will be there:
In the smallest daisies that contain my DNA
and the oldest oak trees that hold my memories.
And in them, I will be eternal.

Jennie Louise is a writer and poet from Hampshire, UK.

She has been writing from a young age but only began to experiment with poetry during her teen years as a form of self-expression. Jennie wrote and self-published her debut poetry collection, All The Things I Never Said, in 2020.

When not writing, she can be found curled up on the sofa with a book and a cup of tea.

www.jennielouise.com

Printed in Great Britain
by Amazon